I0521033

GOD'S DIVINE WORDS CREATE
EMPOWERMENT
FOR THE BODY OF CHRIST
VOLUME 1

Written by
divinewordscreate

Publisher website: www.divinewordscreate.com

For all inquiries: info@divinewordscreate.com

Cover art: The front cover image alone for this book was generated with assistance from AI tools and has been reviewed and edited by a human. For more information on the extent and nature of AI generation for this image, please contact the publisher.

ISBN: 979-8-9938328-0-7

TABLE OF CONTENTS

Foreword

**"In conclusion, be strong in the Lord [be empowered
through your union with Him];
draw your strength from Him [that strength which His
boundless might provides]."
Ephesians 6:10 AMPC**

In the beginning, God created the heavens and the earth.

Those are not just the first words of the Holy Bible, but they truly are a succinct glimpse into the mind, character, and heart of who God is. As the Creator of all things, God has encompassed His desire (mind), His nature (character), and His love (heart) into all whom He has given life to.

As one who creates, you instill within that which you are creating bits and pieces of what is inside of you that makes you unique as an individual.

If you are a musician, you use instruments to produce sounds and melodies from the rhythms that reverberate within your soul.

As an artist, you craft masterpieces with brushstrokes and designs that abound from the depths of your being.

As a writer, you give birth to plots, storylines, and characters that captivate readers' minds while inviting them on a journey into the expanse of your imagination.

What is inside of you comes out of you through everything that you do in life.

It is the God-given ability of man to draw from within in order to give out and give birth to something which never existed before.

What you create is not only necessary, but it is required. And the well from which man draws from is the strength supplied from the presence of God within us which enables us to be able to bring into existence that which was not present before.

When God spoke, He created life. God spoke life into existence by His words—His divine words.

And God said, *"Let there be…"* light, land, seas, vegetation, sun, moon, and stars. What God created was good in His eyes and it pleased Him. This is your same calling in life: to create that which is good in the eyes of God and that which pleases Him.

God has empowered you by bestowing upon you the instruments, tools, and gifts that are necessary to accomplish what He has purposed you for in life.

You have been created by God to:

E- Educate: teaching others with the insight which God has specifically chosen *you* to understand

M- Motivate: inspiring others to reach heights of productivity which will glorify God

P- Provoke: stimulating others while calling them to action

O- Offer: making sacrifices to fill voids in a world which you have been ordained to fill

W- Witness: testifying to others how God's favor and grace has changed your life

E- Edify: build up in a threefold manner- yourself, the Body of Christ, and your neighbors

R- Revere: paying homage to God through acts of worship, love, and kindness

You are a vessel which God is using to accomplish His purposes in the world. God has supplied you with the ability to fulfill His plans through the strength that only He provides.

To think of yourself in any way less than that is to relieve yourself of the responsibility that has been placed inside of you as God's gift to the world through you.

"God's divine words create Empowerment for the Body of Christ" is a series of published works that are geared toward giving clarity and a deeper understanding to those searching for further knowledge of the Bible.

Each chapter examines a certain verse from the Bible and provides a practical look at how one's everyday lives can be guided by Biblical principles.

Divided into volumes, the series is based around the framework of Empowerment.

Volume 1 is **Motivational**. It is crafted to inspire the reader to break out of daily routines and habits in order to reach for their divine calling and purpose.

Volume 2 is **Educational**. It is designed as a teaching tool to captivate the reader's ability to view life experiences from a divine perspective.

Volume 3 is **Leadership**. It is to serve as a catalyst for the personal and spiritual growth of the believer.

"For God's gifts and His call are irrevocable.
[He never withdraws them when once they are given,
And He does not change His mind about those to whom
He gives His grace
Or to whom He sends His call]."
Romans 11:29 AMPC

Ambassadors for Jesus Christ

"So we are Christ's ambassadors, God making His appeal as it were through us. We [as Christ's personal representatives] beg you for His sake to lay hold of the divine favor [now offered you] and be reconciled to God."
2 Corinthians 5:20 AMPC

To be an *"ambassador"* not only means to be a representative or a messenger for someone else. It means that you are of the highest rank. You are worthy. You are esteemed. You are of high regard.

Regardless of your situation or circumstance, you have been ordained, selected, and designated to be Jesus Christ's representative here on Earth.

Many people know what it feels like to be overlooked. As a not-so-great athlete, maybe you were always the last picked in school when it came to sports. Or maybe you felt like the proverbial "ugly duckling" when it came to attracting others.

5

Or possibly you were rejected by family members who did not have the time nor the desire to give you the attention that you so sorely needed as a youth.

But God says to forget about that. He is saying, "You are mine! And I AM all that matters!"

I want you to walk, talk, speak, run, sing, dance, sleep, party, pray, and do every daily task that you do knowing and having the conviction that you are a child of God.

God gives you your identity in Him. You must not let it be dictated to you by man. Your boss at work, your spouse, your government, your Uncle Sam, your president, and all the people who try to box you in and tell you who you are—none of them can brand you or label you. And even if they do, guess what? It doesn't matter.

You were chosen and called by God to be Jesus Christ's highly-ranked representative here on Earth.

And even if you question whether or not you are up for the task, you have a Helper who will guide you to it and through it.

The Holy Spirit lives within you. The Holy Spirit is your Helper. The Holy Spirit is your Advocate. The Holy Spirit is working on your behalf. So let go of your worries, anxieties, and apprehensions.

Decide today; not yesterday or tomorrow. Today.

It's a 4x400 relay race and Jesus Christ ran the first leg. He "crushed the head" of His competitor and gave you a huge head start. He ran that first lap so you would never have to run it.

Now, Jesus Christ is passing you the baton. What are you going to do with it?

How about pick up right where He left off. He laid the blueprint. He laid the tracks. All you have to do is stay on course.

Are you willing?

When Jesus Christ ascended into Heaven, He left work to be done. A lot of work.

Not the kind of work that involves a W-2 or a 401k. But many dependents who need The Message (the Gospel of Jesus Christ). Study the Gospel, learn It, know It, and share It. Share this for all you like. Just get The Message out.

Many are called. Few are chosen. You just happen to be both. Let that sink it.

Someone is waiting on you to pass that baton. It was never for you to hold onto.

God Bless

Call Forwarding

"Still another said, 'I will follow you, Lord; but first let me
go back and say goodbye to my family.' Jesus replied, 'No
one who puts a hand to the plow and looks back is fit for
service in the kingdom of God.'"
Luke 9:61-62 NIV

In this day and age of advanced technologies, we have a
wealth of information and capabilities literally right at our
fingertips. Take cell phones for example. With a single ring
of a cell phone, you can see:

- the number which is calling
- the location where the call is coming from
- the name of the party calling and
- if you have the caller in your address book, a picture
  of your choosing can appear

Along with these visual displays, you also have choices.

Options range from:

1.   choosing to answer the phone call
2.   sending the call directly to a voicemail messaging system
3.   sending a text message response or
4.   forwarding the call to another number

There is also the option of ignoring the call completely simply by not doing anything at all.

You may say to yourself, "I'm not ready to talk to this person right now because I'm in the middle of doing something." Or, "I'll just call them back when I have time or when I feel like it."

So, you forgo it and shift your attention onto other matters.

In this passage in the gospel of Luke, there was a man who was more than eager and willing to follow Jesus' call to him. However, he gave Jesus Christ a stipulation.

He would follow Jesus Christ, the living incarnation of the Most High God, on his own time and when he is good and ready because he has things to take care of. In this particular case, it is saying farewell to his family.

Basically, Jesus called this person and the man hit "Send to voicemail" on his phone.

Unfortunately, it is all too common for most of us to react in the same fashion as this man did.

Our priorities in life tend to begin and end with something other than God. Whether it's the first thing that we do in the morning as we awaken or the last thing we do at night before we go to sleep. There is something that trumps our relationship with God.

When you are at your place of business where you work, you more than likely have a list of tasks and responsibilities that you must complete by a given deadline. If you choose to blow it off to tend to something else, there will eventually be consequences from your superiors.

We can easily understand earthly consequences.

The time is now to discern eternal consequences.

This isn't some Bible-thumping preacher session. It is designed to help you think differently. It is to help put things into perspective for you. And, mainly, it is to empower you.

Our responsibilities at work may come with some sort of benefit or reward if your company is so kind enough. Whether it is a pay raise, a bonus, a promotion, or some sort of recognition for your services.

These are all tangible benefits.

How many of you want the intangible rewards? The rewards that you cannot put your hands on right now but you know they are coming. The rewards that last forever and never tarnish or spoil.

We have many spiritual responsibilities as believers in Jesus Christ. One of the most prominent responsibilities is obedience.

God chooses you! He wants you! He loves you!

If God chose you, He also gave you a choice to choose Him. That choice is up to you. He blessed us with free will to make that choice.

If you know that God is calling you to Himself, think eternally. Believe eternally.

Whatever you think is preventing you from being 100% obedient to that Call is only temporary.

Yes, that job that you are in, even though it has what they describe as "permanent" benefits, is only temporary.

That injury that is bugging you and prevents you from living a normal life; it is only temporary.
That bad relationship that chews up so much of your emotional and mental state; it is only temporary.

When you hear that ring and you look at your phone and it says, *"**Heaven is calling**,"* make that eternal decision and choose to answer and obey. There is nothing else at that moment in time that matters.

Look forward, not backwards. Obedience is the key that unlocks the abundance of life.

God Bless

Dear Abba

"Moses answered the people, 'Do not be afraid. Stand firm and you will see the deliverance the Lord will bring you today. The Egyptians you see today you will never see again. The Lord will fight for you; you need only to be still.'"
Exodus 14:13-14 NIV

Our negative emotions tend to be driven by fear. Whether we face a situation that makes us angry or we face a situation that makes us nervous, our reaction is usually based on fear.

Many times, fear is because of the unknown. We don't know what the result will be so we lash out in anger to try to control, manipulate, or influence the situation so that the outcome will be in our favor.

If someone happens to upset you (or if you even think that they will upset you), you may try an intimidation tactic by showing how riled up you can get.

Or, if you have a timid nature, you may react submissively as to not "ruffle any feathers."

In both scenarios, fear is the nucleus.

Have you ever noticed how a young child may fall down and scrape his or her knee? The child doesn't start to cry immediately. The child may look around first to see if their parent or someone else saw or noticed what happened.

Or, the child may look at the actual cut on their body if there is one.

Then, and only then, will the child begin to cry.

The child thinks:
"Help me! This cut really doesn't hurt too much but I'm so disheartened that I fell and no one was there to protect me."

We are that child in adult form.

Life Choices
Everything in life is a choice. Everything.

Whether you go outside and walk with the crowd or you go outside and skip around like you don't have a care in the world—it is all up to you.

And so is how you respond to the situations in your life.

Hardships happen to everyone. If you're saved, you are not exempt from hardships. In fact, yours may be even more trying than the average person of this world.

The difference is you have a Parent who not only can, but will, fight your battles.

One sign of spiritual maturity is knowing when to say or do nothing at all. If you will just have the conviction that whatever situation that you're going through is too much for you to handle, just confess it to God. Simple as that.

You were not invincibly made, physically or emotionally. You have your limitations.

Thankfully, God doesn't.

If God says that He will fight your battles, believe Him. After you believe Him, thank Him. After you believe Him and thank Him, just get out of the way—His way and your own way.

Too many times, we think that we share all the attributes of God.

Well, here is some good news: We are not Omnipotent.

Our "power" is limited to how much our Father, Abba, has allocated to us.

You can do all things *through* Christ who strengthens you.[1]

That means that you need help. And there is nothing wrong with needing help when you have a Father who has limitless power for our limited lives.

When you give it to God, you can now interpret the words of Moses and apply it to your life as, "For the 'Trials and Tribulations' you see today, you shall never see again."

In the Book of Exodus, the Israelites, who were so blessed to have the promise and shielding of God, simply had to believe. We, as the Body of Christ, share this promise and shielding of God today once we gave our lives to Jesus Christ.

All we have to do is believe Him for it.

Whatever issue you are facing in your life right now, it is time to take hold of that stress and be done with it. Take hold of those fears and put them behind you. You were not made to fight every battle. Sit this one out on the sidelines.

Like the child in need wanting help from his daddy, we are to turn to our Dear Abba and ask Him to have His way.

Tell yourself that you're taking a step back and that step back will actually be a step of faith. You are no longer relying on yourself. You're relying on the One who gave the Promise.

Watch as those fear cells inside your body turn into faith cells day-by-day. You'll feel more alive. You'll feel rejuvenated. Your thinking will change.

God has got your back. You are going to press on regardless of your circumstance and regardless of your situation.

"Abba" signifies closeness, intimacy, and a presence that is not bound by distance. Therefore, when we call on Abba as our dear Father, we are affirming that our relationship is loving, nurturing, and protective with full assurance that the providence of God will guide and lead us for the goodness of His holy name.

Have a change of perspective today realizing that our Abba is near and watchful. He is aware of your every need. Never abandoned or neglected, our dear Abba will see you through.

God Bless

Uncover Your Talent

"And I was afraid, and went and hid your talent in the ground. Look, there you have what is yours."
Matthew 25:25 NKJV

We live in a segmented world. We, as well as our governments, political and world leaders, tend to group us all. From the haves to the have-nots, upper class to middle and lower class, rich to poor, skilled to unskilled, employed to unemployed, etc. The list goes on and on. We all fall somewhere into those categories.

As believers, we learn that in the beginning, God gave Adam dominion over every living thing on the Earth. Adam was instructed to be fruitful, multiply, fill the Earth, and subdue it.[2]

We also learn throughout the Bible that Jesus was to reconcile us back to God to the way God intended things to originally be when He created Adam.

Adam was given 3 things:

1. dominion
2. clear instructions and
3. the responsibility to be obedient

Gifts

To the male readers, have you ever received a funny-looking tie or some cheap cologne on Father's Day? To the female readers, have you ever received knockoff jewelry or half-wilted flowers on Mother's Day?

Or have you ever received something on your birthday that you just threw into the closet never to look at it again?

Not to suggest that you did not want any of those things. You just either didn't like them or had no use for them.

You sincerely appreciate the kindness from the one who gave it to you. But you really didn't know what to do with it.

When you are Born Again, you are a new creation. You are heading toward what God initially intended in Adam.

Yes, it is a journey and doesn't happen right away. But you start anew.

And with this fresh start, the Holy Spirit begins to reveal certain things to you.

One of those things is the revelation that you, like Adam, have dominion. No, it is not expected of you to rule all the things on the Earth.

But you do rule the gifts that God has given to you.

You choose and decide how to use what God has given to you. You did not have this revelation before. You do now.

The Holy Spirit reveals to you that what you have, all that you were given, and all good things come from God.

Multiply Your Talents

The parable in Matthew 25 is about three servants who were given talents (think of it in financial terms for a minute).

The first was given a certain number of talents (currency/money). He took those talents, doubled it, and returned it to his master.

The second was given less than the first but he also took it, doubled it, and returned it to his master.

The third was given less than *both* the first two but he hid it in ground.

He then returned to his master exactly what he was given. Nothing more and nothing less.

He said he did this because he was afraid.

Do you remember Adam?

Adam, after disobeying God by eating from the Tree of the Knowledge of Good and Evil, hid in the Garden because he was afraid.

Are you connecting the dots?

Many of us are afraid that if we let go of our grip on what we have, that we will just collapse. The trust is not there to know that God will lead us and provide for us in any and every situation.

God gave you gifts, talents, and abilities to take them, invest in them, increase them, and then return them back to Him *and* His Kingdom with more than you were initially given to begin with.

Like the obedient servants, we are to use the talents that we are blessed with to honor and glorify God.

The disobedient servant who hid his talent in the ground had that very same talent taken away from him by his master and it was given to the obedient servant.

Conquer Your Fears

Adam was instructed to subdue.

Like Adam, we are to conquer our fears of not having enough.
We are to conquer our fears of losing everything.
We are to conquer our fears that the Lord won't provide.
God has and God will.

Like those segmented categories that we all fall into, it doesn't matter where we fall or how much we have or don't have.

We are to use what we do have for God's purpose.

Even if it is less than the person next to you or less than the rich man or less than the "haves." What matters is what we do with what we are given.

Take your skill, whatever it may be, and say, "I am going to use this skill that I was given to glorify God. I am going to use this skill that I was given to serve."

I don't care if it is even frying an egg.

If you're skilled at frying an egg, fry some eggs for a homeless or hungry person and serve them *in God's name.*

If your skill is shopping (yes, some of you have made a skill of it), give your excess clothes away to the needy *in God's name.*

25

If your skill is playing music, play music for the sick at hospitals and hospices in your local community to cheer up their day *in God's name.*

Do not for a second think that you can just sit on what you were given and accumulate it for your own good and your own needs.

We are servants. And obedient servants reap the rewards of their obedience.

God Bless

The American Dream

"No, I am suggesting that what the pagans sacrifice they
offer [in effect] to demons (to evil spiritual powers) and not
to God [at all].
I do not want you to fellowship and be partners with
diabolical spirits [by eating at their feasts].
You cannot drink the Lord's cup and the demons' cup.
You cannot partake of the Lord's table and the demons'
table."
1 Corinthians 10:20-21 AMPC

Many of those who currently live in the United States of
America either have distant ancestors who migrated there
from another country or they themselves came from another
country. If you were to ask them why, common answers
would be:

- for a better lifestyle
- for more safety
- for a better education
- for more opportunities or
- to attain "the American Dream"

You do not have to be from another country to chase the American Dream.

It is an *ideal* or a *mentality* that you hear about from a very early age: house with the white picket fence, stable job, family and children, and an all-around swell life.

There is nothing wrong with having dreams and goals and striving to attain them. We all would like to live in a certain way and live a certain lifestyle.

In fact, setting goals and having the discipline to accomplish them can create an immense spirit of achievement. You've done it. You've reached the apex, the pinnacle, the top of the mountain.

Reasons for Sacrifice
This verse in 1 Corinthians reflects on sacrifice.

Sacrifice involves offering. When you sacrifice, you are basically giving something up. It could be anything. Something which you have you end up having less than when you first started all because you sacrifice it.

No one gives anything up without a reason. And that reason is crucial. It is key. It is the nucleus. It is the core. That reason is the center of everything that revolves around it, depends on it, and relies upon it.

The reason *why* you sacrifice is what needs to be focused on.

That reason is the blood in your body.

That reason is the oxygen in the air that you breathe.

That reason is the gas in your car that allows it to drive.

You cannot do anything without that reason.

What is that reason for a believer?

That reason is: your faith in God. And it is and should be the foundation of your life.

Your body cannot function without blood means that your body cannot function without faith in God.

You cannot breathe, and hence, live without oxygen in the air means that you cannot breathe, and hence, live without faith in God.

Your car cannot drive without gas means that your Christian walk cannot mature and blossom without faith in God.

Sacrifice for a Purpose

An idol can be anything or anyone that you put before God. It can be something tangible or intangible. It can be a person. It can be a dollar bill. It can also be a lifestyle.

If I put a glass on the highest shelf in the kitchen cupboard and someone shorter than me reaches for that glass, they may have to go on their tippy-toes to reach it or twist and contort their body to get to that glass.

They are sacrificing gravity in the process. So, there's a risk involved. They risk falling, hurting themselves, or even accidentally dropping things that are in proximity to what it is that they are reaching for.

They are giving up something that they had at the beginning with both feet planted firmly on the ground to try to get that glass which is just out of reach for them.

To attain it, they must make a choice.

That glass can be the American Dream. Or that glass can be God's purpose for your life.

But in no way, shape, or form can that glass be both of them.

The American Dream was not given to you by God. The American Dream is *of the world*. The American Dream caters to the world. The American Dream satisfies the thirst of the world.

God's purpose for your life is *divine*. And like that glass, it may be out of reach.

But it is attainable.

"Give and it shall be given unto you." [3]

Sacrifice and it shall be sacrificed unto you.

God, not the world, supplies all your needs.

When you sacrifice your family, your morals, your love, your convictions, and your faith chasing the dreams of this world, you are like that short person reaching for the top of the cupboard but knocking everything down in the process.

Everything around you will eventually suffer because the base that you are standing on is shaky ground.

It is not stable. It is not reliable. It is temporary—temporarily constructed and temporarily standing.

You are a believer. And when you are a believer, you don't have to reach around hoping to grasp the glass (God's purpose for your life).

You're supposed to bring over a chair and then stand on that **Faith** to get to the glass!

Jesus told Peter, "On this Rock I will build my church." [4]

The Body of Christ will be built on faith in God. And that's always solid ground. That's permanent ground. That's eternal ground. That's everlasting ground.

31

You cannot split your time and split your allegiances.

You cannot sing praises to God in church on Sunday and then dance with the devil at work on Monday.

These are not one-time sacrifices to God. These are eternal sacrifices, eternal offerings, and eternal choices.

We are giving up now the desires of the flesh and the desires of the world in faith to reap the abundance that He will completely supply.

The dinner table is prepared and the Living Water is yours to drink.

There is only one glass to choose that will quench your eternal thirst.

The choice is yours.

God Bless

Passing the Test of Life

"All has been heard; the end of the matter is: Fear God
[revere and worship Him, knowing that He is] and keep
His commandments, for this is the whole of man [the full,
original purpose of his creation, the object of God's
providence, the root of character, the foundation of all
happiness, the adjustment to all inharmonious
circumstances and conditions under the sun] and the whole
[duty] for every man."
Ecclesiastes 12:13 AMPC

There are many tests throughout one's life.

If it's not an examination related to schooling, it's a test
related the examination of your health. Or it could be a test
of your patience, your tolerance, or even a testing of your
nerves.

We go through the test, do our best, and hope to hear the
results from those in charge of administering the test.

All tests can be prepared for.

- In school, you can study or cram for an upcoming test.

- If it is a medical test, maybe you must fast or make certain changes to your nutrition and diet prior to taking the test.

- If it is a test of your emotions, I'm sure you've had plenty of opportunities in the past to respond to a situation in a certain way knowing full well that things will go either good or poorly based on the way you chose to respond. Basically, you know what works and what does not work.

The Test of Life is no different.

We Are Prepared to be Tested

We are prepared to take the Test of Life. We are fashioned by our circumstances. We are fashioned by our situations.

We go through our entire lives dealing with things that may be foreign to some but are all preparation for us to take that Test of Life.

We see people have gains in life and enviously ask the question, "Why did *they* win the lottery?"

We witness people have losses in life and sympathetically ask the question, "Why did *that* person have to die so early?"

Ultimately, these end up being the seeds that germinate and develop into the life experiences that prepare us for this Test.

There comes a time after you are born again where you start to come into right relationship with God. You think differently. You act differently. You desire differently.

The things that may have appealed to you prior to you being born again just don't appeal to you in the same way.

Well, they shouldn't seeing how you are a new creature and a new creation.

We can go through life with different jobs, different relationships, different homes, and different everything.

But there should always be one constant: the conviction within you that you are a new being.

We Are Purposely Tested

Like a surfer riding a wave that starts in the middle of the ocean, the surfer must move with purpose.

Try to ride the wave too soon and you will likely get swallowed up in an explosion of water.
Try to ride the wave too late and you will likely just fizzle out with no solid foundation to move steadily on and make progress.

Like the surfer, our Christian walk must move with purpose. The journey, like the wave, has peaks and valleys. We will crash and burn at times. We also will drift awkwardly with no solid footing.

But through it all, we are to acknowledge God for who He is.

As that new being and that new creation, we are to hold God in the highest regard with the fear, reverence, and awe that He deserves.

No one and nothing should ever come before this. It is your responsibility as a believer. It is the only answer that you will ever need for the most important test that you will ever take.

So, when those waves of life come crashing in and you question how can you go on or what should you do now, the answer is always the same.

When those gains and losses occur, we turn back to our purpose.

When those changes in life happen with your job, relationship, etc., you always know the answer to this Test of Life.

You've prepared for it. You've studied for it. It's now a part of your new genetic makeup—your new Christian DNA.

We Are Equipped to Pass the Test

No matter what I am going through, my feet are grounded in Who I believe in.

No matter how hard the tide is crashing in, my fear is not of the wave.

My focus is on Him who creates the wave.
My respect is in Him who gives the wave its power.
My amazement is in Him who I know will guide me through it.

My jaw doesn't drop at the magnificence of the wave itself. My jaw drops at the sight of His hand that will steer me and lead me through this wave.

My mouth will not scream in fear of the wave. My mouth will shout praises of thanksgiving to Him who cares for me so much as to not allow the wave to swallow me up.

What am I here for? What is my purpose in life?

You are surfing your way to heaven with a smile on your face and joy in your heart, dipping and dodging obstacles, falling and getting back up, always keeping focus on the One who is smiling back at you with joy in His heart knowing that you passed the Test and is ready to give you your reward.

God Bless

Against His Will

"And Saul said, 'Who are You, Lord?' And He said, 'I am Jesus, Whom you are persecuting. It is dangerous and it will turn out badly for you to keep kicking against the goad [to offer vain and perilous resistance]'."
Acts 9:5 AMPC

As in all our lives, there have been those times where things simply did not work out as we hoped they would for ourselves. Things just didn't go "according to plan."

Whether it was a relationship which you were hoping to start or a job opportunity which you knew you had locked up— somehow and some way it just didn't work out.

Confusion sets in and sometimes disbelief. You wondered why when you aced the interview or you just knew that the guy/girl of your dreams was a sure thing.

Along with confusion and disbelief, emotions such as anger and sadness can push themselves through making you a total wreck in the process.

But what about those times when things did go your way? Have you ever had them?

You made your plan, put your best foot forward, and *Voilà!* He or she said, "Yes!"

Or you landed that job with the increase in salary and things are working out just as you hoped they would for you.

We all have those victories in life where we get what we set out for.

Contrary to the negative emotions of anger and sadness, in these scenarios we feel overjoyed and happy.

Our plan. Our victory. Our joy. Our happiness.

Our Will and Our Purpose

**"Like the cattle that go down into the valley [to find better
pasturage, refuge and rest], the Spirit of the Lord caused
them to rest..."
Isaiah 63:14 AMPC**

When there is a group of livestock (cattle, goats, sheep, etc.)
and they are out in the field, they graze what is available to
them which is usually the grass that is right in front of them
within their proximity.

We've all heard the expression, *"the grass is always greener on the
other side of the fence."*

Well, there is always that one animal who begins to wander
off in search for that greener grass—that pasture which it is
sure tastes better than the one which it is currently feeding
on.

Usually, one goes and then the rest of the herd follows after
them. Now, you have a bunch of wandering cattle and some
farmer or the owner of the cattle who must go, gather them,
and then bring them back home to where he needs them to
be.

Since these cattle are not domesticated and there are many of
them, he needs to have a way to *guide* them.

To do so, this owner uses what is called a ***goad***. A goad is some sort of stick or pointed object that he can use to guide the cattle into the direction that he needs them to go in.[5]

Now, this goad is not pleasurable. I don't think you or I would like to be poked and prodded with some object. So, we can safely assume that the wandering cattle do not like this goad.

When we push forth chasing our plans (the plans that we came up with by ourselves and for ourselves) but we do not consult with God first, sometimes He will give us exactly what we are seeking and exactly what we are asking for.

However, the sustained results are not always as joyful as we had anticipated them to be.

God's Will and Plan for Your Life

God chose you to be His own before you even existed. His plan for your life was set into motion.

God may allow you to go your own way for a period of time. However, there will come a time when He needs you to follow His plan for your life.

A dilemma occurs when we resist because of our own desires and we choose to seek what we want for ourselves.

When God has called you, the Holy Spirit acts as your conscience. There feels like there is an urge and a desire within you to do certain things or to even avoid certain things.

That is the Holy Spirit working within you. That is your *goad*. That is God loving you, wanting you, and needing you to take directions from Him.

In Acts Chapter 9, Jesus told Saul that it would not work out favorably for Saul to kick against the goad and to keep working against God's will and plan for Saul's life.

The same applies to us when we make choices in our lives to chase after what we want and what we believe is best for ourselves.

God may allow us to have our temporary victory. But, if we are not where He needs us to be, He may have to get our attention by poking and prodding us to get us onto His path just as the wandering cattle need to be goaded and guided back on course.

As believers, we cannot be "occasionally Christians" who profess to believe in God yet go our own ways, not trusting Him for who He is.

We must be 100% full-time Christians knowing and believing that God is our Provider.

We must ask the Holy Spirit to help us to trust God's plan for our lives and to give us the conviction to surrender our lives completely over to Him.

We tend make plans for ourselves with the safest options.

But we need to get to the point where we allow ourselves to let go and let God reveal His plan to us knowing that He is our safety net and we can always trust Him to catch us if we fall.

We tend to resist God's plan for our lives because there is risk involved.
"How will I manage? How will I stay afloat?"

Jesus told His disciples to go, preach the Kingdom of God, heal the sick, and to take nothing with them.[6]

That is not a request. Those are divine instructions.

They are divine instructions that lets them know that their needs are already met. As their Provider, He is the One who brings the Provision.

Whatever and wherever they are, there is no need to worry because He is the one who gives.

The path for our journey is laid in Faith. All we have to do is believe God for who He is.

You are empowered to succeed and have an impact in this world. Your work today can have a lasting effect on others for years to come.

The Body of Christ functions as a whole and you have been chosen to play your part. Don't resist and settle for the painful prodding that comes when you choose to wander down your own path.

Choose God's path.

The herd may follow each other but you were created to listen to your Master and to obey.

Let God know that you want to fulfill His plan, to celebrate His victory, to give Him the glory which will bring your joy and your happiness.

God Bless

They Don't Understand Our Relationship

"And the scripture was fulfilled that says, 'Abraham believed God, and it was credited to him as righteousness,' and he was called God's friend."
James 2:23 NIV

One of the classic American comedic television shows, *The Odd Couple*, was about two roommates who were polar opposites.

One was a neat freak and very meticulous.
The other was pretty much carefree and not so concerned about appearances and order.

The juxtaposition of the relationship between these two roommates is what created the necessary synergy and laughs for what turned out to be one of the best TV shows of its time.

The **judgmental** side of human nature looks at the "odd couples" of the world and wonders things like, "How did they ever get together?" or "What does she even see in him?"

Along with sayings like "You are a reflection of the company you keep" and "Birds of a feather flock together," it is easy to fall into the trap of prejudging without looking deeper into the relationship of the individuals involved.

On a surface level, it does not appear to be a match.

Have you ever seen someone question another person's success or accomplishments before?

It happens frequently in the world of sports. Take any Olympic games' Track & Field competitions for example.

If someone happens to just obliterate a long-standing record finishing time in an event, some will automatically whisper suggestions of performance-enhancing cheating by the winner. Due to the history of the sport, some skepticism may be warranted.

However, it is possible that the person or team took the necessary steps in training in order to reap the rewards at the finish line.

God's Relationship with Abraham

God and Abraham have a personal relationship. Abraham is God's friend.

A friend is someone you trust.

A friend is someone you care for.

A friend is someone who knows all about you yet still likes you and still wants that connection with you even despite your flaws.

Shouldn't we all strive for that? I cannot speak for you, but we should all want the closeness with God that Abraham had.

Was there some secret, magic formula that Abraham possessed to have such a bond with the Almighty?

Maybe Abraham prayed five times a day.

Maybe he fasted.

Maybe he followed rituals.

Or maybe not.

Abraham was a man who had many things in life. He had abundance.

The Bible reveals to us that Abraham was a man rich in livestock, silver, and gold. He had servants who worked for him.

Abraham even had a beautiful wife named Sarah. She was so gorgeous that Abraham once told her to lie to the Egyptian king to say that she was his sister, fearing that he would be killed if it was found out that she was his wife.[7]

There are many rich men in this world who have money, cars, a beautiful wife, and possessions. We see these people all the time—on TV and even in person.

They have the things that can make others jealous.

Some will spend their entire lives chasing what these people have.

Some will even compromise their morals and ethics in the process just to get it.

But then there's Abraham—someone who already had so much. He had plenty of material possessions. But he lacked just one thing: a child of his own with Sarah.

Oftentimes, we like to pat ourselves on the back and give credit to ourselves for what we have worked so hard for and the things that we have come to attain. We will say to ourselves, "I put the work in and I deserve the credit."

The spiritual reality and fact is that all good things come from God. All gifts and all that we have are not detached or separate from God.

God promised to give Abraham that one thing that he lacked. And not only would He give it to Abraham, but He was going to give Abraham so many descendants that they could not even be numbered.

That "secret, magic formula" was simply Abraham believing that God would do what He said He would do and being faithfully obedient to Him in waiting.

There was no reason for Abraham to give credit to himself because the credit came from God. And it was righteousness.

Abraham's faith in God brought blessings that superseded those surface-level appearances of abundance that his peers and the world would look at.

Abraham's money, wealth, and possessions would not come close to matching the never-ending blessings that God would bestow upon him.

It is the eternal blessings that would make others envious of Abraham's relationship with God.

Our Relationship with God

Has someone ever tried to knock you off your course and somehow you just seemed to bounce back and be better than you were before?

They will sit back and wonder, "How did you make it? How did you get there? I thought you were done. I thought you were finished."

Your former employers will question, "We laid you off from your job and now you're flourishing in life?"

Ex-partners will be surprised thinking to themselves, "I dumped you and now you look better than ever before?"

They simply don't understand our relationship with God! The world is confused how we can thrive when everyone thought we would be finished.

As a believer, you are favored.
As a believer, you have divine privilege that is only reserved for a few—a chosen few.
As a believer, you have Grace that saves you from all of the pitfalls in life that can knock the average person down.

We don't chase after what the next person has.
We wait with anticipation and expectation for the rewards that we believe through faith are rightfully ours.

So, while the judgmental stares of the world wonder in amazement how we can smile in the face of adversity, our faith, like Abraham's, keeps us in right standing with God.

The poor, the hungry, the sick, the ones who lack but still turn their attention toward the God Who provides will forever keep the world guessing as to what God sees in them.

God sees your faith in Him and it is time to let the world start seeing it too.

God Bless

Statute of Liberty

*"In [this] freedom Christ has made us free [and completely
liberated us]; stand fast then, and do not be hampered and
held ensnared and submit again to a yoke of slavery [which
you have once put off]."*
Galatians 5:1 AMPC

In the first ever race of the Indianapolis 500 in 1911, Ray
Harroun was a driver with a disadvantage.

In those times, racecar drivers would drive with a riding
mechanic who would ride alongside the driver of the vehicle
and keep the driver informed as to where the competitors
were in relation to their car.

On this particular day in 1911, Harroun was without a riding
mechanic. So, he took a mirror and mounted it inside of his
racecar so that he could see all that was going on behind him.

This was the first use of a rearview mirror mounted in a car.[8] Ray Harroun went on to win the race.

As with racecar drivers, we all use rearview mirrors today while we are driving. It helps us to make decisions like when to change lanes, when to speed up, and when to slow down.

Freedom in the Past Without God
Can you recall your life prior to you being saved?

For many, it was a life of fun. Maybe it could be described as a life of "pleasurable recklessness."

That may sound like an oxymoron but valid nonetheless as it depicts a time when consequences may not have mattered much to you.

You would do whatever it was that you desired because there was some enjoyment in it.

Maybe you drank too much or partied too much or even associated yourself with not the best crowd of people.

You drove in the fast lane. Like Harroun in the Indy 500, there were not many who could keep up with you.

Or maybe your life was simpler. Maybe you weren't a "party animal" but you made choices and decisions without involving God.

God was the furthest thing from your mind when it came to living life.

Maybe you knew of God but did not really care about how He felt about what you were doing.

Many of us have been there.

Philippians 3:7 (NLT) states:

"I once thought these things were valuable, but now I consider them worthless because of what Christ has done."

When Jesus died on the cross, the veil was torn. No longer was there a boundary between us and God.

Jesus was that extension of God.

Jesus was, and is, the link in the broken chain.

And it is Jesus who has given you this new freedom.

You have been set free—freed from your past and freed from the penalties of sin through Christ.

Whatever demons had you in bondage no longer have power over you.

Become Free in the Present
Both believers and unbelievers drive with rearview mirrors.

The difference between the two is that unbelievers are enticed and hunger for what they see behind them.

Unbelievers are intrigued by what they see in that mirror. Past bad relationships, past addictions, and past vices all affect how an unbeliever conducts their lives.

An unbeliever will fall victim to the pleasure of past satisfactions.

They will look in the rearview mirror at cars driven by *Greed* and *Idolatry* and actually slow down for them.
They will change lanes to allow cars driven by *Lust* to drive right alongside of them.
They will speed up to chase cars driven by *Jealousy* and *Envy*.

But the believers—who are the chosen and called children of God—ride with the Holy Spirit.

The Holy Spirit along with the Word of God forces us to keep our eyes on the prize.

There is no need for us to remain fixated on what transpires in that rearview mirror of our lives.

It doesn't move us and it doesn't shake us. Our focus remains on the road ahead.

Just as Paul urged the Galatian churches of his time to remain strong and not succumb to the rituals of the past Law but to grasp onto the freedom given by Jesus, we too, as the Body of Christ, must stay focused on our new life.

A potter who crafts a beautiful figurine does not long for the days of shapeless mounds of clay. He adores the beauties and endless possibilities of His new creation.

A Race for Freedom
The Indy 500 is a 500-mile race which consists of 200 laps.

This means that you will have plenty of opportunities to drive next to and around your competitors: your old habits, your old associates, and your old demons.

But you are to leave them exactly where Ray Harroun left them—stuck in your rearview mirror.

Your faith in God has given you the power to stay the course that you started when you gave your life to Jesus Christ. So, don't turn back.

Ask God to allow the Holy Spirit to strengthen you to say "No" to those past distractions that try to creep into your new life, cut you off, and knock you out of your lane.

Push on towards that final lap while the angels cheer you on and wave the checkered flag of liberty.

You have been called to freedom.

Let us rejoice in faith and celebrate the victory that we as believers are destined to receive.

God Bless

Spiritual Selfie

"Wives must not let their beauty be something external.
Beauty doesn't come from hairstyles, gold jewelry, or
clothes.
Rather, beauty is something internal that can't be destroyed.
Beauty expresses itself in a gentle and quiet attitude which
God considers precious."
1 Peter 3:3-4 GW

If someone were to hand you a shovel and told you to dig
into the ground, could you do it?

I'm pretty sure you could dig for a few *feet* through the grass,
then through some soft soil, and then deeper into the ground.
Not far, but you could manage to make some headway to a
couple of feet.

How about if someone handed you a shovel and told you to
dig between 90 and 190 *miles* into the ground?

After stopping yourself from laughter, you would probably pass on the request knowing full well that you did not have the tools to do such a task. Clearly, a mere shovel would not be able to take you that far.

If one were to dig 90 to 190 miles into the ground, past the Earth's crust, beyond the Earth's mantle, and into the Earth's core, there you would stumble upon what are known as diamonds.

We all know what diamonds are. We've seen them. We wear them. They are every girl's best friend—or so I have heard.

But diamonds are not easily accessible. They are hard to come by.

And things that are hard to come by are usually more valuable than those things that are readily available.

No matter how spotted or dirty it may be on its surface, even the smallest diamond has value when it is mined from deep inside of the Earth.

And besides, a diamond can always be cleaned up, shined, and polished to remove those things that hide its luster.

The Outward Selfie

In this day and age of technology where so many people have access to cellphones, we are in the midst of the "selfie" phenomenon.

As most know, a selfie is where one takes a picture of themselves.

With so many outlets available, it is quite the norm to take a picture of yourself and upload it onto one or more of the countless social media platforms out there. Selfies are quite the trend.

The interesting aspect of selfies is that it is never usually the first picture of yourself that you choose to put up. Maybe your head was turned at the wrong angle or you didn't like your smile or your hair didn't look so good.

So, the solution is to take as many selfies as possible to find the best ones to post to your friends and all of the world. You want to look your best, right?

That first selfie picture that you snapped, the one with all of the flaws, is just like that dirty diamond that was excavated from the Earth.

On the surface and at first appearance, it was not thought to be good enough.

The Spiritual Selfie

We are spiritual beings. Our bodies are just houses for our spirit.

The Bible describes our bodies as an earthly tent.[9] A tent has layers just like the outer crust and mantle of the Earth before you can reach the diamond beneath.

The diamond does not shine on first contact.
If you pull anything out of the dirt, it will be messy.

But just like our lives as believers, we shine after we are cleaned up. That polishing occurs when you are Born Again.

Your value to the Kingdom increases just like the value of the diamond goes up when it is prepared to be put on display.

Your beauty isn't shown in the fourth or fifth selfie you took to appear just right for the camera.

Your beauty is within as God looks toward your spirit.

Your character, your convictions, your beliefs, your morals— these are the traits that sparkle and glisten. These are the traits that are everlasting and cannot be destroyed.

Express that beauty in humbleness of spirit just as Jesus, Who had all and could do all, humbled Himself in obedience all the way to the cross.[10]

Let your Spiritual Selfie be displayed by how you conduct yourselves in your everyday lives.

Even if you are caught off-guard, the first picture of you is always a good one because it is who you really are.

You are the diamond that doesn't need to be covered up or buried.

God sees past your clothes, your makeup, your fashion sense, and all the superficial layers on top of who you really are.

Let God and the world see the beautiful qualities of your nature. Your real nature. Your spiritual nature. Not an artificial nature that is just for show.

The Authentic Selfie

Synthetic, or "man-made," diamonds are formed in a laboratory (think: cubic zirconia). In order to be made, they are subjected to enormously high temperatures and high pressure.

Although nice-looking on the exterior and pleasing to look at, these synthetic diamonds are not the real thing.

We all know what happens when you subject something to high pressure situations. They tend to crack, fold, and not hold up.

But as a child of God, you are authentic. You are authentically loved and authentically made.

Your spirit was made to withstand the intense pressures of the world through God-given faith and it is that same faith that needs to be put on display.

Shake off that dirt and grime that the world tries to bury you under and shine brightly like the diamond that you truly are.

You are of high value, high worth, and are highly-esteemed.

No longer a diamond in the rough, flash a smile for God's camera. You are His prized possession and beloved exactly as you are.

God Bless

Sphere of Influence

"A man's gift makes room for him, and brings him before great men."
Proverbs 18:16 NKJV

If I were to grab one end of a penny-sized rubber band (it has the circumference to fit around a penny) and you grabbed the other end, there would only be a limited amount of force which we could use to pull this rubber band in opposite directions before it eventually popped.

We would have to be careful pulling on our respective ends because we both know that when a rubber band pops, it is capable of hurting either or both of us as it snaps.

If we both pull and pull but decide, however, to stop before it snaps, the rubber band will still be intact but it would have expanded a bit and be stretched out more.

Elasticity is what allows an object to be stretched like the rubber band but still retain its shape despite some force being applied to it.

A rubber band has elasticity. It may be limited in the case of the rubber band, but it has elasticity nonetheless.

Our penny-sized rubber band has expanded and can now fit around a larger coin like a nickel, for example.

Your Trusted Sphere

If you were to examine your life and had to quantify how many people are affected by what you do, would it be a fairly small or large number?

For many of us, it may be our immediate family (spouses, children, and siblings), a few trusted friends, and maybe a couple of co-workers. Please don't count your social media friends as "trusted" friends because how many of them can you really trust? We're talking on a more intimate scale.

Now that you've thought about it, first take your immediate family as an example.

They are obviously affected by your day-to-day decisions because there is some sort of dependency there.

They rely on you just as you rely on them. They rely on you for love, affection, sheltering, financial support, etc. and vice versa.

Your trusted friends may turn to you for advice, a listening ear, or comfort during trying times.

Your co-workers are affected by your presence and your output on the job.

So, you've built up a nice amount of close people that are well within your reach. These are the people that you love and care about.

But have you ever stopped and wondered about those who may not be in your reach? Have you thought about those who are not in your vicinity or who you do not correspond with on a daily basis?

Sphere of Stewardship
God has given us gifts and those gifts must be shared with others.

We tend to think that what is ours belongs solely to us.

The *Stewardship Principle* teaches us that nothing is ours. We are managers. We are caretakers. We don't possess anything.

And if God gave you something, He for sure did not intend for you to keep it all for yourself.

He chose you over someone else to have it.

God knows that you have the capacity to responsibly manage what He has given you.

Your heart is like the rubber band. And it is your choice to either hoard God's gift to you for yourself and your penny-sized collection of immediate family, friends, and co-workers or you can increase your sphere of influence and share His gift to you with the world.

God has equipped your heart with elasticity.

Through the stretching and pulling of life's difficult and trying circumstances, God has expanded your heart and enlarged your territory.

No longer is your loving and caring only confined to those who are around you. You have the ability and the responsibility to reach as many people as your heart, not your hands, can touch.

When you use what God has gifted to you for His purpose, you don't have to worry about limits or restrictions.

Your gift will open doors for you. Your gift will unlock opportunities and possibilities for you.

Where once you could only hold onto what was right in front of you, God works to create more space in your life for outreach in areas that you may not have even imagined.

Sphere of Giving

We must put away penny-sized thinking and the doubts about what we convince ourselves that we cannot do and cannot accomplish.

We must move forward to gain access to the networks that God has unlocked and will make available to us.

What once was just a circle of acquaintances now grows into a community of fellowship, helping and sharing common interests amongst each other.

God's gift will take you beyond what is familiar and routine to you *if* you are willing to allow His grace to lead you there.

Your love, your affection, your comfort, and your output all can be shared with a far greater audience and fulfilling far greater needs than you knew they could because now your circumference is much wider.

If you have ever felt satisfied after being thanked by one person for lending a listening ear, just imagine ten, twenty, or one hundred or more people thanking you for answering a prayer of theirs that you never even knew that they prayed about.

That is the effect of you sharing your gift.

You are God's vessel of grace and what better day than today to start giving some of what you have been blessed to receive.

God Bless

On Their Behalf

"And the Lord restored Job's losses when he prayed for his friends. Indeed the Lord gave Job twice as much as he had before."
Job 42:10 NKJV

In criminal trials in the United States of America, individuals are protected by the Fifth Amendment in the Bill of Rights. It states that:

"No person...shall be compelled in any criminal case to be a witness against himself..." [11]

It is your right against self-incrimination. So, in other words, this Fifth Amendment of the U.S. Constitution protects you from you. It gives you protection from the proverbial "putting your foot into your own mouth."

This is more commonly known as, *"pleading the Fifth."*

As a defendant in a criminal case, you can refuse to take the witness stand under the rights given by the Fifth Amendment in hopes that you would avoid saying something that might be used against you that proves or confirms your own guilt.

It sort of prevents you from testifying against yourself.

It is quite the norm in high profile cases for defense attorneys to advise their clients to plead the Fifth in order to save themselves from being found guilty. The assumption here is: the less you say for yourself, the less likely the chance that the words you speak will end up hurting you in the long-run.

On Behalf of Ourselves

The Bible introduces us to a man of the highest profile by the name of Job.

A rich and influential man, Job had it all. Not only was Job blessed with material wealth but he was highly-favored by God. So favored that God spoke of how proud He was of Job's honesty, integrity, and righteousness to none other than Satan himself.[12]

A person would have to be mighty special and dear to His heart to be singled-out by God in such a way.

So special in fact that God *ordained* Job to have to go through hardships and loss because He felt that Job was strong enough to handle them all.

Stripping Job of his children, possessions, and health, God *permitted* Satan to torment Job in the most torturous of ways.

Job was a man who used to be the talk of the town and well-respected because of how set apart he was by being showered with so many blessings. But he was now a man who was shunned, mocked, and ridiculed by the very same people who used to admire him so much. No longer esteemed by the public, Job was crushed to have to go through this all.

However, instead of turning to God to find comfort, Job relied on three of his friends. He looked to these friends to give him answers as to why all of this was happening to him.

Although they were considered Job's friends, these three people blamed Job for his own calamities. They professed that it was Job's sins which caused God to punish him in such terrible ways even to the point of saying that Job was paying for the sins of his own children.

They stated that this is how God works.

To them, this was God's retribution—God's way of making Job suffer because of the acts that Job did and did not do.

And they could not have been more wrong in their reasoning.

The Holy Spirit Acts on Behalf of Us

In Job's haste to prove himself to God and to turn things around for himself, Job lost himself in the process.

Job wanted to confront God. He wanted to know firsthand from God what he did wrong and why he had to suffer since he was such an upstanding man.

In his mind, Job must have thought, "Since I am so blessed and highly-favored, why God are You punishing me when Your punishment should be reserved strictly for sinners?"

Job questioned God's motives. Job questioned God's intentions.

You see, we tend to mistake God's discipline for punishment. And we tend to confuse God's refinement for retribution.

A potter cannot make a figurine without first putting the clay through the fire.

And it is not the role of the clay to question his Maker and Molder as if the clay is the one who is in control.

Through God's Omniscience, He knew that when He allowed Satan to torment Job, that Job would not curse God.

However, God also knew that Job would question why he would have to experience this since he was in such right-standing with God.

Job got away from who he always was.

When Job's children would party in all of their lavishness and have fun, Job would make sacrificial atonements to God just in case they had sinned or cursed God in their hearts.

Job would *intercede* to God on their behalf because it is when we are praying for others that we become Christ-like.
It is when we put ourselves secondarily that we love like Jesus.
It is when we take a step back to bring others forward when we emulate the characteristics of God's only begotten Son.

When we intercede in prayer on the behalf of others, we are mirroring the Holy Spirit who pleads our case to God on behalf of us.

The Holy Spirit acts as our defense attorney advising us as God's children to be still and allow Him to speak for us in ways that we could only imagine doing for ourselves.

There is absolutely nothing wrong with prayer requests and supplication for yourself.

However, it is in the advanced stages of spiritual maturity when you can take your gift of access to God through prayer and use it to benefit someone else by interceding and being that mediator for them when they are in desperate need of a blessing.

We have all been saved, healed, helped, and blessed because someone was praying for us and we didn't even know it. Someone right now is praying for your protection, your prosperity, and your upliftment.

And, we as believers need to take hold of the power of intercession and know when it is the right time to *"plead the Fifth."*

We need to recognize when it is the right time to not testify against ourselves but to *bear witness* on behalf of someone else for their gain and for their betterment.

We are to Intercede on Behalf of Others

Job lost himself when in the face of disaster, he went away from the traits which kept him righteous, the traits which kept him consecrated, and the traits which kept him set apart.

When Job questioned God's treatment of him, God confronted Job with disappointment.

God had to remind Job who was the Sovereign One.

It was in this moment where Job immediately realized the error of his ways and repented.

Job's three friends who lied about God and misrepresented who God really is could have severely faced the brunt of God's wrath. But God showed mercy and instructed Job to pray for them.

Just like how Job would always pray for his own children, Job interceded on the behalf of his three lying friends and God accepted Job's prayer for them. They were spared because of Job's mediation.

So, it wasn't simply their sacrifices to God that saved the three friends, but it was the obedient intercession of God's child that saved them.

You have that same power. Grace allows you to do just as Job did.

And when Job prayed for them, God restored to Job all that he had before.
And not only did God restore it, but God doubled it.

Today, harness the avenues and outlets that you have been so richly blessed with to use.

Join the Holy Spirit in a circle of prayer as you are being prayed over and as you pray over someone else's life.

Life is not just about what we ourselves go through but what we *all* must go through.

Make it a habit to plead to God for someone else as badly as you want blessings for your own self. You may be surprised by the return that you receive being more than you ever imagined.

God Bless

Return On Investment

"...having also believed, you were sealed in Him with the Holy Spirit of the promise, who is a first installment of our inheritance, in regard to the redemption of God's own possession, to the praise of His glory."
Ephesians 1:13-14 NASB2020

They say that when you purchase a brand-new automobile, the value of it declines as soon as you drive it off the lot.

Research shows that a new car depreciates about 10% the second you take it into possession as your own. Not only that, but the car's value will decline anywhere from 8% to 12% every single year.[13]

The thinking behind this is that, as the years go by, factors like wear and tear on the car, the age of the car, the supply and demand of newer cars, as well as other factors will make your old car less valuable and less attractive to potential buyers.

Your car now has less trade-in value. It is no longer worth a premium after having been marked up for sale when you initially bought it.

If the person who sold you the car wanted to buy it back, they will see a *profit* since they would get it for cheaper than what you originally paid them for it.

And you, on the other hand, would have suffered a *loss* since you would be receiving much less than how much you paid when you first acquired it.

Return On Investment ('ROI' for short) is a measurement of performance. Anything that you invest in can be gauged by how much was put into it and eventually over time, how much was gotten out of it.

From stocks. to real estate, to automobiles, and many other things of value, ROI can be analyzed to determine the efficiency of those investments. In other words, if one needed to assess the benefit of making a choice between one investment over another, you could use the ROI to compare and decide which one has the highest potential and would be worth making an investment in.

About that new car you bought, you know realistically that you cannot keep it forever. You know that eventually you will probably have to get rid of it and upgrade to a newer and better version.

You also are fully aware that all cars depreciate even though you have a plan of selling it later on. You want your Return On Investment to be as high as it possibly can be.

So, instead of driving the car into the ground, you decide that you are going to take good care of the car. You are going to wash it twice a month, use the highest grade of gasoline, and be careful not to scratch the car if at all possible. This car is your prized possession and nothing is going to get in your way of keeping it as pristine as you can.

In fact, not only do you want to keep your car in tip-top shape, but you want it to be just as good, or if not better than the day you first bought it.

So, when the tires get a little worn out, you replace the tires with new and improved ones. But, instead of the *standard* tires that the manufacturer gave you when you originally bought the car, you now get All-Season tires which are best used for driving in different types of weather and terrain.[14]

And when the windshield wipers leave streaks on the glass and clouds your vision, you get beam-blade wipers which are more advanced than conventional wiper blades.[15] The sleek beam-blade wipers function more effectively, are more durable, and are better equipped to withstand any inclement weather conditions which you will have to navigate through.

And for those dark and foggy days and nights where your standard headlights limit your visibility and depth perception, you opt to go with Xenon headlights. These are high-intensity discharge headlights that emit a very powerful, yet clean white light which makes objects like reflective highway signs and road surface markings shine more brightly. These lights are so strong that they are capable of blinding oncoming traffic.[16]

So, instead of just sitting idly by while your car ages and breaks down throughout the years, you invest your time, effort, and energy ensuring that when the time does come to recoup what is yours, you will get your just due.

And how wonderful it is to know that God treats His own children the very same way.

God's Investment for Eternity

As God's eternal children, we are not some standard model that gets run into the ground only to be thrown into the scrap heap at our end of life. No, that scrap heap is reserved for those who do not accept Jesus Christ as Lord.

We are God's precious children who are chosen for succession.

Not only did Jesus Christ stand in the way, but He gave Himself up as God's collateral for us. And through His death, God has invested in us day after day, month after month, and year after year.

Jesus' death and resurrection allowed the Holy Spirit to serve as God's initial deposit into our future.

Receiving the Holy Spirit is the first installment in a lifetime's worth of upgrades, maintenance, and re-tuning of our lives.

When our legs are weary from traveling along our spiritual journey and our spirit is low, God gives us new wheels to walk on that can withstand every storm in our way.

For we as believers know that to everything there is a season.[17] And who can persevere through slippery snow and rain without being equipped with the proper tools to carry you through those treacherous conditions? It is God who pours into us the high-octane fuel that we need to press on.

And when your vision for the future becomes cloudy and you want to pull over to the side of the road to give up, it is God who provides clarity and makes your paths straight when you trust in Him with all your heart.

It is by His Grace that all of the distractions, debris, and obstacles are removed from in front of us so that we can proceed on in faith, hope, and confidence believing that we will make it safely to our eventual destination.

And when the dense fogs of life try to put limits on how much of the magnificent future that we can envision for ourselves, it is God who shines high-intensity Light on His righteous children.

It is God's Word that is a lamp to our feet and a light to our path.[18] He makes His signs clear to us so we know which road to take when we are tempted to go the wrong way. He shines a Light so bright that even darkness cannot comprehend it.[19]

So, over the course of your lifetime, you are constantly being made better, made whole, and made useful for your eventual renewal.

As His children, you are being prepared by God to be redeemed for God.

And there is nothing that can equate to His Return On Investment in you because it is all for gain.

What a joy it is to know that God's devotion and dedication to your upkeep is reserved only for those who believe in Him. And what a joy it is to know that we will not be run into the ground but constantly built up because God believes that your value to the Kingdom was worth the premium that Jesus paid for it.

You are God's choice—a much more worthwhile investment than another.

Realize that you are the highest-rated blue chip performer in His portfolio.

God Bless

For All Intents and Purposes

"Do nothing from factional motives [through contentiousness, strife, selfishness, or for unworthy ends] or prompted by conceit and empty arrogance. Instead, in the true spirit of humility (lowliness of mind) let each regard the others as better than and superior to himself [thinking more highly of one another than you do of yourselves]. Let each of you esteem and look upon and be concerned for not [merely] his own interests, but also each for the interest of others."
Philippians 2:3-4 AMPC

"*For all intents and purposes*"—this is an expression that is used when describing things which are not exactly 100% alike but have enough in common to align their similarities.

For example, a person could state:
"The one baby twin has a mole on her left cheek and the other baby twin has a mole on her right cheek. But for all intents and purposes, the twins are identical."

In this case, the twin baby girls are not exact replicas of each other (no two people are) but they have enough major characteristics in common to be classified as identical.

If we break the expression down, *intent* is something that directs your actions. When you intend to do something, there is something compelling inside of you—whether in your mind or in your spirit, but definitely in your character—to do something for an expected reason. You want 'X' to be done because you are expecting 'Y' to be the result of it.

- You hug someone because you *intend* to make them feel comforted.
- You become a doctor because you *intend* to care for the sick to help them become better.
- You make a donation to a charity because you *intend* to meet someone's needs.

There is a reason for your action. There is a goal in mind for your action. And the result of the reasons and goals of your actions is your *purpose*.

It is why you are doing what you are doing.

The Poor Farmer

There is a poor farmer who owns acres and acres of land. His only crop is grain. These are high-quality grain. However, the poor farmer does not have the means to grow his grain on all of the land that he possesses as it would be too much labor and far too costly for him. The amount of grain that he yields is just enough to feed his immediate family.

One day, the mayor of the town stops by the farm. He is impressed by the quality of the grain so he approaches the farmer. He offers the poor farmer a substantial amount of money if the farmer would agree to mass produce these grains. The mayor would provide all of the tools necessary so that grain can grow over every acre of land on the farm. The only stipulation is that the farmer would have to agree to have potentially harmful pesticides sprayed across his crops to protect the growth of the grain.

On the one hand if he agrees to go through with it, the farmer would no longer be poor. Also, he would not only be able to feed his family but many others as more grain would be produced than ever before.

But on the other hand, the effects of the pesticides would damage some of the grain in the process. And, the use of pesticides would also adversely affect the wildlife in the area who feed off the crops and it could possibly contaminate the water.

Many times in life, we are faced with decisions that test the merits of our character. And it is our intentions that are at the root of our character. You may have an end goal and purpose in mind that is of some benefit. But it is your intentions and the means by which you go about fulfilling that purpose which reveal what is truly in your spirit.

As believers especially, we must take a deep look into the reasons *why* we do the things that we do.

As an aspiring young adult, you may make a commitment to spend years in medical school with the intention of one day becoming a doctor and caring for the sick. But if the primary motivation for you entering this field is the lure of potential riches and that lure supersedes your desire to aid those in need, then your purpose for caring for the sick becomes secondary. Taking care of the sick simply becomes a byproduct of you being a doctor. It is not your purpose in life.

Benevolence takes a backseat to greediness.
Selflessness gives way to selfishness.

And these are not the characteristics of those who seek righteousness.

For what appears on the surface to be identical to something that is good, at its core is something that is actually tainted.

And this is the lesson that Jesus taught us in the parable of the wheat and the tare.[20] The sower's good crop of wheat gets overrun with tare (weeds) which were planted by the enemy. The tare is similar in nature to the wheat. The tare appears to be exact replicas of the wheat that it grows alongside of. Society will have us believe that for all intents and purposes, they are the same.

But God knows which one is His. He knows which one He has planted. He knows what the driving forces are inside of them, stimulating them, and causing them to grow.

We don't seek to imitate God's character, God's principles, and God's way of life with the intention of gaining for ourselves.

Our purpose in all that we do should be to serve others. And in doing so, God will take care of our growth. He will cultivate the areas of our life that may presently be barren but will become fertile grounds that are ripe for good seeds to be planted.

When we make sacrifices humbly for the benefit of others, the cost and the burden are not ours to bear alone.

Good intentions do not always produce good results.

The poor farmer may intend to feed more people but his crops are corrupted.

A doctor may intend to care for his patient but if the doctor's motives are not pure, then his patient will ultimately suffer.

Godly intentions yield righteous results.

When we shift our reason for doing things 'for *all* intents and purposes' to doing them 'for *Almighty* intents and purposes,' we will gain the proper perspective to make the right choices and decisions in our daily lives.

Make that change today, examining your own life and what it is that you currently do.

No job you do should just be a paycheck. It should first and foremost be an act of service that you do with purpose. The world desperately needs more like-minded laborers because as Jesus put it, "the harvest is plentiful but the workers are few."[21]

So, don't allow the world to confuse you with counterfeit Christians who appear on the surface to be just like you but at the root of their character is nothing but an imitation of who God calls us as His children to rightfully be.

Pray for the conviction and the obedience to do all things for God's intentions and God's purposes and watch as He raises you up to be the standard for all others to emulate.

God Bless

Social Engineering: The Phishing Reel

**"'Even the priests and prophets are ungodly, wicked men. I
have seen their despicable acts right here in my own
Temple,' says the Lord."
Jeremiah 23:11 NLT**

Even the most skilled fishermen know that heading out to
sea is an adventure filled with unknown mysteries and
outcomes. Anything can happen journeying out on the rough
waters so it is always best to be prepared.

It would be unwise to voyage into the vast lakes, seas, and
oceans without the proper equipment, tools, and strategies to
not only have a safe endeavor, but also a productive one.

From life jackets to food supplies, it is best to venture out
with the mindset that anything can go awry. Your hope is that
you have all that you need to make it a successful outing, but
you want to ensure that you have taken the necessary steps
to protect yourself, those who you are with, and whatever it
is that you are hoping to catch.

You cannot be consistently successful at catching fish without a rod and reel. And you cannot preserve your catch long-term without ice and a cooler. Depending on the size of the boat that you are on, more may be needed if, for example, you are expecting to bring in a larger haul.

Larger fish need larger storage. A small boat will only require standard-sized coolers filled with ice. The bigger the boat and expected catch, you will need a huge freezer which has more capacity that can potentially be filled.

The average fisher who does it for leisure or as a hobby may only bring the minimum essentials to catch their fish. A rod, reel, and bait are suitable to get the job done.

However, a fisherman who does it for business as their livelihood knows the tricks of the trade. Besides, how would they be able to compete with other fishing businesses if they only carried the same tools as a hobbyist? There are more factors which these types of fishermen need to account for.

The power required to haul in the fish correlates with the weight of the fishing rod and reel. To catch smaller fish, it is best to use a lighter rod. To catch larger fish, a heavier, more durable rod is necessary. It takes less effort for fishermen to reel in a small fish because they don't give as much resistance. Therefore, there is less pressure on the rod and less effort is required by the fishermen to reel their catch into the boat.

A longer rod and reel also have more reach and can be cast much further into a body of water.

The Lure of Bait

Every fisherman knows that fish are an elusive species. And it would be a futile effort to attempt to try to catch fish without using any bait.

Fishermen use bait to lure fish onto their hook. The sight, sound, and even smell of the bait used all play a role in attracting fish to get their attention. Bait is used to mimic the characteristics of food and prey. It is used to entice the fish in hopes of getting them to bite. From the movement of the bait to the vibrations which the bait causes in the water, fish become allured by the guise of what appears to be beneficial to them.

Fishermen use bait as a deception tactic to target gullible fish. But even innocent fish simply looking for a meal may find themselves on the wrong end of a fishing hook.

Phishing for Trouble

As a technological term, "*phishing*" is a practice employed for malicious intent to trick unsuspecting users into believing that something is coming from a trusted source when in fact it is not.

Phishing is a social engineering attack which uses deceptive methods for fraudulent purposes. Those who engage in phishing seek to gain access to personal information, money, and systems by impersonating known, trustworthy, and reputable parties.

For example, you receive an email which appears to be from your bank so you open it, click on a link, and enter your password and personal information. Unbeknownst to you, the sender misrepresented who they were. Although they used the bank's name, logo, and identity, they were actually criminals who were putting on a front to give the appearance of legitimacy. What you thought was a safe space turned out to be infiltrated and corrupt. By giving them access, you unknowingly exposed all that you have to bad actors.

Phishing mimics the characteristics of fishing by using the same techniques to function effectively. The perpetrators first seek out who is available to be caught, then they get their attention, and finally they lure them in. They may not be able to trick everyone because some are aware of the methods which they use to operate.

To avoid phishing attempts against you, it is critical to practice 'Zero Trust.' Essentially, this means to "Never trust, Always verify."

You are to never blindly trust someone or something without verification. You are to observe and confirm that what is being presented to you is indeed credible. You cannot make assumptions or feign ignorance. You must teach yourself to be wary. It is the spirit of discernment that will help you to protect yourself.

Not everyone has intentions of doing good. There are mischievous plots and schemes out there seeking to capitalize on another's innocence.

A Chosen Few

Jeremiah the Prophet was one of the few people in the Bible who God spoke *directly* to. As the son of a priest, it was Jeremiah whom God told:

> *"Before I formed you in the womb I knew you, before you were born I set you apart. I appointed you as a prophet to the nations."*
> *Jeremiah 1:5 NIV*

Even though he was young at the time and felt ill-equipped and ill-prepared, God had to let Jeremiah know that he was in fact chosen, sanctified, and ordained for God's purposes. God had laid out plans for Jeremiah's life before he even existed. God ordered Jeremiah's steps before he even took his actual first steps.

God called Jeremiah to be a prophet. Jeremiah was to be a spokesperson for God to enlighten, instruct, and warn.

This was not Jeremiah's choosing. We can assume due to his apprehension that he had plans of his own. But he was called by God. And through obedience, Jeremiah answered that call.

Jeremiah wasn't cosplaying the role of a prophet—he was legitimate. Therefore, his words and actions could be trusted.

As a prophet, Jeremiah's words would be true—because they were spoken from God.
His predictions would come to pass—because they were foreshadowed by God.
His guidance should be adhered to—because they were commanded by God.

Unlike Jeremiah, there were false prophets in the land. They dreamed their own dreams and thought their own thoughts. Their visions were their own. They were not God-inspired nor God-sent, but they gave people the *appearance* and the *impression* that they were speaking the words of God. The same can be said of the priests and elders who sat in high places but in reality, were far from God.

It was common for priests and false prophets to wield power over those who were searching for answers. Their positions gave them influence in the community. They spoke with authority. They exuded confidence. Their words were convincing and believable.

When people are hungry for direction, meaning, and purpose in life, they are like fish in the water.

They hunger so they search.
They thirst so they seek.
They desire so they chase.

And they will be lured by that which seems beneficial for them.

The Intentional Church

The false prophets and priests who had the ear of the people relished in their positions of power and influence.

As those who should be entrusted with the oracles of God, false prophets did not hear from God but rather spoke lies in His name.

As shepherds established to lead according to the Law of God, the priests actually led people astray based on their own rules of conduct.
As overseers of the flock of God, they watched over them with a covetous eye.
And as ministers of the Temple of God, they did not uphold the sanctity of His house.

In fact, it was the house of God in the Gospels where Jesus was referencing *back* to Jeremiah, condemning that it was no longer esteemed as a house of prayer.

99

> **"'Has this house, which is called by My name, become a den of thieves in your eyes? Behold, I, even I, have seen it,' says the Lord."**
> **Jeremiah 7:11 NKJV**

It detested God that the very place which was set aside for the glory of His holy presence was not maintained with the reverence which it was due.

When Jesus flipped over the tables of the money changers and those who sold doves in the temple, He felt anger, disappointment, and exasperation.[22] What was taking place in God's house was *not* how God intended for it to be.

Have you ever wondered why multiple chapters in multiple books of the Bible are dedicated to such intricate and specific details about the construction of God's house—from measurements and dimensions to the types of materials and utensils to be used and placed inside of it?

Maybe God was emphasizing how dearly it meant to Him to share this intimate space with us, allowing us to bask in the magnificence of His glory. His Temple was God extending Himself to us—a sacred place so holy that you were both literally and figuratively forbidden to exit out the same way in which you entered in.

It meant something special to God. Therefore, it should mean something special to us.

And now the representation of His Temple being our houses of worship today—the churches and synagogues which we go to—are grander than ever. Some are being constructed with profit and gain in mind. They are being built bigger to hold more and expanded to do more. Larger fish need larger storage.

The hearts of the leaders of some of these *institutions* have been compromised and they are more driven by the quantity of God's reward rather than the quality of God's relationship. They have put on outwardly the identity and name of a Christian to give the appearance of piety while internally they seek to build their *families'* kingdom on the foundation and basis of God.

Some preach prosperity. Some preach legalism. Some have even gone so far as to twisting the words of the Bible to justify the abuse of children.

Christianity has unfortunately been overrun with 'phishers' of men.

This is not an attack on the church.

It is a mirror being held up for the Body of Christ as a whole to see its own reflection.
It is a call to demand more transparency from these leaders and to cultivate more awareness by these congregations.

The stark reality is that the actions of a few have turned off and turned away many who are seeking and searching for the Truth.

Reclaim your name as a Christian from those who have misused it. Protect your reputation as a follower of Christ from those who seek to confuse it. And restore the sanctity of the house of God from those who have misappropriated it for purposes other than the glorification of God.

God Bless

VOLUME 1

motivational [moh-t*uh*-vey-sh*uh*-nl]:

inspiring or seeking to inspire people to act in a certain way,
especially so as to overcome obstacles and achieve success,
happiness, etc.[23]

Footnotes, citations, and references

1. Page 18: Philippians 4:13 KJV
2. Page 21: Genesis 1:28 NKJV
3. Page 31: Luke 6:38 KJV
4. Page 31: Matthew 16:18 NKJV
5. Page 42: "Goad." Merriam-Webster.com Dictionary, Merriam-Webster, https://www.merriam-webster.com/dictionary/goad. Accessed 16 Oct. 2025.
6. Page 44: Luke 9:3 NLT
7. Page 50: Genesis 12:12-19 KJV
8. Page 56: Richard McCuistian. "A Brief History of Automotive Mirrors." Carparts.com. July 12, 2024. https://www.carparts.com/blog/a-brief-history-of-automotive-mirrors/
9. Page 64: 2 Corinthians 5:1 NIV
10. Page 64: Philippians 2:8 NIV
11. Page 73: National Archives. "The Bill of Rights: A Transcription." Archives.gov. Last reviewed August 7, 2025. https://www.archives.gov/founding-docs/bill-of-rights-transcript
12. Page 74: Job 1:8 NLT
13. Page 81: Victoria Scott. "Understanding Car Depreciation." U.S. News & World Report. May 27, 2025. https://cars.usnews.com/cars-trucks/advice/how-does-car-depreciation-work
14. Page 83: Automotive Training Center. "All-Season Tires Versus High Performance Tires." 2025. https://autotraining.edu/automotive-tips/tires/
15. Page 83: Brake & Front End. Sponsored by ANCO Wiper Blades. "Beam vs. Conventional Wiper Blades: Which is Better?" October 5, 2022. https://www.brakeandfrontend.com/beam-vs-conventional-wiper-blades-which-is-better/
16. Page 84: Rick Popely. "Xenon Vs. LED Headlights: What's the Difference?" Cars.com. December 26, 2020. https://www.cars.com/articles/xenon-vs-led-headlights-whats-the-difference-430847/
17. Page 85: Ecclesiastes 3:1 AMPC
18. Page 86: Psalms 119:105 NKJV (verse also referenced on back cover)
19. Page 86: John 1:5 KJV
20. Page 91: Matthew 13:24 AMPC
21. Page 92: Matthew 9:37 NIV
22. Page 100: Matthew 21:12 NKJV
23. Page 103: "Motivational." Dictionary.com Dictionary, https://www.dictionary.com/browse/motivational. Accessed 16 Oct. 2025.